Whoopeee!

Written by Teresa Heapy

Illustrated by Joanne Partis

I was skipping up and down, when
Fred ran up to me. "Wait!" he said.

"I have to whisper something."
Then he said, "I can yell and ..."

"Whoop! Whooperoo!"

Ow! My ears were ringing.
It was a trick! I did not like it.

At lunch, I was munching a snack,
when Philippa ran up to me.

"Oh, I have to tell you something,"
she said. "I can go ..."

"Whee-whizzeroo!"

Oh, what a shock, again! My ears
hurt. This was no fun.

Then, at the park I was running and kicking. Finn ran up to me.

"I have to tell you something," he said.
"It is something just for you!" So, I
bent down next to him, and he said ...

"Whackeroo! Wham!" He went
stomp, just like an elephant.

I was cross. I had to think ...

Then they all said to me, "Come on!"
Their grins were big. "We have one
extra thing to tell you."

"Oh no," I said. "I have something
to tell you! You think I am afraid,
but I can go ..."

"Yahoooo!"